The Inside of an Orange

Also by James B. Golden

Sweet Potato Pie Underneath The Sun's Broiler (2009)

Afro Clouds & Nappy Rain (2011)

The Inside of an Orange

Poems by

JAMES B. GOLDEN

iUniverse, Inc.
Bloomington

The Inside of an Orange

iUniverse books may be ordered through booksellers or by contacting:

iUniverse
1663 Liberty Drive
Bloomington, IN 47403
www.iuniverse.com
1-800-Authors (1-800-288-4677)

ISBN: 978-1-4759-4765-6 (sc)
ISBN: 978-1-4759-4767-0 (hc)
ISBN: 978-1-4759-4766-3 (ebk)

Library of Congress Control Number: 2012916505

Printed in the United States of America

iUniverse rev. date: 10/24/2012

For Hazel and Henrietta—

This collection is dedicated to the life,
artistry and legacy of Whitney Houston.

I'm an orange moon, reflecting the light of the sun.

—Erykah Badu

O Lord, my God, I cried unto thee, and thou hast healed me.

—Psalms 30:2

Contents

Why Are You Forcing Me To Eat Vegetables?

The Inside Of An Orange

Introduction

Oranges are varied—sometimes sweet, sometimes tangy or bitter even. They're the most human fruit.

The Inside Of An Orange is a cornucopia of thought.

It's about healing. It's about spiritual growth.

This collection of poetry gives anecdotes and quivers of our greatest experiences.

It begins with a discussion on artists, resistance, and Blackness. I wanted to give the world some hope, while staying close to my artistic cadence as a writer of truth. The second section of the book is more comical and lighthearted, while the final section wrestles with spirituality and heavier social issues.

These poems are funny, at times reflective, inquisitive, celebratory, spiritual, but always real.

There are many influences present in this work including: Charles Bukowski, Erykah Badu, Langston Hughes, Nikki Giovanni, Sylvia Plath, and the amazing Whitney Houston.

In fact, memories of Whitney, my greatest muse, are scattered throughout the book and her spirit permeates its pages. (See note in the *Acknowledgements* section)

My grandmothers are strong women, and having to see them battle Alzheimer's disease has added to the depth of this project. Their spirits have christened many of the poems in this work.

When I began writing *The Inside Of An Orange*, I had just gone through therapy and released a bunch of depressing poems to the world. I wanted to celebrate the emergence of a happier me—someone who could finally laugh.

While these particular poems are open and whimsical, there are serious moments and reflections on heroes who have come and gone.

The socio-political undertones of the poems are intentional, providing a backdrop for a greater historical conversation to take place on race, disease, gender, sexuality, rape, and introspection.

I want readers to feel good after reading *The Inside Of An Orange*—blessed, actually.

Feel like you have the ability to do anything because of the people and events which provided the fuel for change.

This book is an exposition of emotion meant to challenge everyone to *live supernaturally*, ultimately inspiring our very best selves.

James B. Golden,
October 2012

An Artist's Requiem

A Better-Looking Me

I've got my smile back.
The skies have opened
for me.

No more darkness-covered soul
feeding my mind
sour tuna fish sandwiches and
rotten mayonnaise.

My smile is bigger than coke.
It's higher than dope.

I am up up up
in the sky
joyful as a dancing sun.

I've become a finally
better-looking me.

I Love You, Black Man

You are big
and bold—
and I love you,
Black man.

Your fists are bigger
than the ocean,
lips stick out
like mama's
butt.

They speak the sounds of
someone superbly saxophone
by nature—
soulful

and I love you,
Black man.

I love you,
Black man!

I love you,
Black man.

Son Of Obama

I'm a Son of Obama.
We bump the same beats,
hitting the dancefloor to Jay Z
tune the tube to TV One,
Centric, VH1 Soul, Planet Groove—
those classic BET shows.

We play basketball on
Saturday mornings, before
briefings begin on foreign affairs,
spending just enough time before
tea.

I'm a Son of Obama.
Brown skin liquid in the sun,
dripping down the sides
an ice cream cone.

Our hair matches hues.
We attend the same barbershop
same Soul-Glo classic fade,
razor trimmed edges.
We gossip, cracking jokes
only father and son
discern.

I'm a Son of Obama.
Up tall in solidarity,
especially when he believes
everyone is an equal.

He raised me up over
his head to a thunderous applause,
Leo presents cub.

He anointed my head with oil.
Shine, shine for the world
to see.

I'm a Son of Obama.
He looks just like me.

My Blues

Let's keep all options open,
while we sing our blues.

A dash of alliteration
pinch of salt
cup of improvisation.

The voice will beat beat beat
across the staff,
crying all over the keys.

My blues will grow before us
leaving flotsam along the
seashore.

Think Like A Writer

Get your weekly dose
enjoy the insanity
spend time eating it.

Upgrade your morning routine,
think like a writer.

Erase all the rules
mark your territory on ledger
always store away the drippings.

Dare to be beautiful
instantly
walk with all gall
have a pen,
have a ball.

An Erykah Badu Poem

I am a lyric
from the pages of history.

Beyond witches and warlocks,
nature and love.

I'm from an Erykah Badu poem!

I picked from apple trees
forbidden and woke up
to tell you the time.

Carried your bags that
they wouldn't weigh down
so monstrously—
you kissed me on my neck.

I fell in love with
a bumblebee and tasted
her honey.

Named a building
after you,
and spelled it correctly.
Erykah's "ykah" threw
some off, but not me.

Lord knows I'm trying,
to open
penitentiary gates,
set free the me's inside
the shell.

I sit often beneath
orange moons,
letting light
tell the time.

Many many many nights
I listened to crickets
underneath the snare
and cymbals.

They comfort me.

The hi-hat made love to me.
I said "how good it is".

I am flow,
phat beat—
jammin'
laughin'
singin'
talkin'
speakin' from inside
the speakerbox.

I praised God in there
and she loved me quickly.

I was written and
expressed in the voices of
Chaka and Mayfield—
half Diana, one part Stevie.
Whitney was always in there
and Billie orchestrated them all.

Gil Scott baptized me
Jill—my prayer partner.

I'm brighter in you.
I appear on a
better looking type
of paper.

I smile with my words—
take breath away.
Store words in the
hidden place of seed.

I am boundless
more honest than tea,
better with side dishes—
wholesome enough alone
to eat.

I am flow, song, lyric.

I am he and she,
and she's always
in me.

I Was There

For Amy Winehouse

I was there Amy,
with you.

My veins turned purple, black, blue
stuck up with poisonous medicine
healing that busted heart.

I saw you pass out on stage
those heated Brazilian
nights when the heroin seeped
through your pores dripping down
a thunderous crash on the
barren stage floor.

I was there Amy,
in the audience when
we first heard that voice
a magnificent overture of strings
and woodwinds.

You died under our skies
and we let the rain
pour.

I was there,
dropped tears
into the soil of
a tattered soul.

Consumption Lifestyle

Up and down sides
people walk and
stomp like they have
places to go.

Across and under
bridges and overpasses
common bums lie
awake waiting for
sleep to come.

The homeless are
absent of image, even
the brassy trumpet sits
in the distorted distance.

The Song Donna Summer Never Sang

ooooh . . . .
you're so good
you're so good
you're so good
you're so good

because you are.

Dozens of hits
crystal pipes
beaming over techno beats

you're so good.

ooooh . . . .
I feel love
I feel love
I feel love
I feel love

When it rained the ceiling
turned the color of licorice,
red strobe lights piercing green eyes,
trapped in your
disco.

My head twirls—
little gyrating top.
I can wait to
come down,
though.

I can feel good
with you.

I feel love
in you.

I feel love.

They Don't Have To

I step foot in a
gas station,
the stares start.

Side eyes open from the
potato chip aisle,
prying into my skin.

I see them judge me.

They don't have to
say anything.

Freedom's Gate

For NAACP, SNCC, BPP, and the SCLC

I wear bite marks well
around my ankles and thighs.

The water hoses couldn't
wash away
my fire
burns steadily
encased in cement blocks
guarding my soul.

Dogs punctured
but did not break
my bones.

I called called called
to the heavens
relieve us below
and God sent
a ride-or-die ability
to cause hell on earth
for any who chose to
stand between
me and freedom's gate.

JAMES B. GOLDEN

I'll walk in one day,
over the mountaintop.

I'll jet ski down that
beast—
right into the light.

How I Became A Feminist

I believe Uncle Luke did it.

Nelly helped.

So did Ludacris.

Somewhere around
"big booty hos" and
"splash waterfalls",
my feminist water
broke and flooded all those
pens and papers.

"We don't love dem hos"
christened me and
shook me down to my knees
praying for God to free me
from this everlasting exploitative
emergency.

Code Blue
on my TV screen!
Womanity's dying
all around me.

Domestic violence subsets
the ghetto and
mass Chris Brown-like crimes
saturate the inner scope
of my blatantly urgent
need to
rescue these beauties
from the deadly crisis
created by the hands of
pacifists.

I will no longer
forward these striking
male fists
to those who populate
our census lists,
and this poem may
put me on a blacklist
but this opportunity will
surely not be missed

to call them queens
our most sunny days
gospel songs
charming beautiful
goddess unicorns
our ladies
are flagrantly all of this
and most divinely,
the shit—

dismissed.

The Day Michael Died

No calls
please.

No emails
internet's shut down.

Three sleeping pills
in the afternoon
a glass of water
"hope I'm out soon".

Head touches pillow
teardrops forming puddles
water wells
eye bags blow up.

Irregular heartbeat
beating a spoiled drum
fade to darkness,
no more sun.

A Fine Composition

For Nick Ashford

I know these things happen
and it must be true
that artists come
and they leave too.

You were here yesterday
and gone today
took some of our
Soul-session piano
away.

We'll miss those glassy haunting eyes
long jet black frock
towering genius
standing on his tip tops.

I'll play your songs often
and speak of you to children
about your love for art
for Soul music.

A fine chocolate masterpiece
and dozens you've given
to those simply starved by
ultra-bland rhythms.

You were here yesterday
and gone today
took some of our
Soul-session piano
away.

Remember me as a sunny day
remember me as he who played
songs that rose a generation
from the pits of hopelessness to
unspeakable gladness.

God, those Marvin and Diana
dusties were classic.

An ability to convey through lyrics
love for a Valerie Simpson
who bore your children
made us listen

her all-inclusive range
and Soul-laced pain
love unconfined
baptized in rhyme

christened by your touch
on those old craggy keys
in a Hitsville basement
with the rest of our Kings

and Queens alike
singing the greatest
out-right defiant
love-struck composition giants.

I looked away for a minute
stared too long at a sun ray
lost a stone from my temple
flattened out to clay.

You were here yesterday
and gone today
took a bit of our gold
retracted the bold
moved forward from our
pound the keys
till they burn down the bridge
and light the muthafucker
on fire
heyday

took our Soul-session piano
away.

Rahsaan's Blues

He begins with the bass line
lyric then melody
bluesing us all over
instruments and musical spaces
stretching his chords far
across the sea
changing seasons,
fell in love too early
with Rahsaan's Blues.

Rhythm
cultivated before any
words slip from his lips
greasing our skillets
sautéing the meat,
coloring our experiences blue,
Soul crayons
packaged in
piano key boxes.

He's been down in the pits
with us,
our blues sound the same—
recalling Nina and Buddy,
Etta, Solomon
deep down at the bottom

of the bayou,
penetrating minds,
baritone notes impregnating
our ears.

We didn't ask for
commercialism

he never gave it to us.

It was always
always
from the gut.

Rahsaan has been blue
for time spaces
beyond comprehension
the deeper his soul grows
the richer his blues get.

Frozen Me In Time

Me, oh, my
woke up in fright
opened up eyes
looked to the night
you said goodbye.

Your absence has
frozen me in time
like melting ice sculptures
on wedding nights.

3 years I've seen you here
now I've gone blind
looked to the sky
you said goodbye.

Excuses, excuses
have blown me dry
paper towels soaking grease
from fries,
stopped breathing tonight.

Son absent from my eyes
spent hour-glassed time
you said goodbye.

JAMES B. GOLDEN

An Artist's Requiem

You were a butterfly
in most spaces.
I didn't allow your
colors to flourish vividly
in the sun.

Sorry for that.

You were foxier
than them,
but life
makes a fool of an artist
sometimes.

I'll paint another,
but it won't be you.

The Whitney Houston Suite:

Wonder If You Can Hear Me From Heaven

Make it.

I'll make it.

One day like you,
somewhere on the
other side of the sky.

Free from the
lingering smoke of a
heavy burning town.

Rest eternal,
dissolving sorrow like
powder washing machine
detergent.
Colorful as crayons,
sweet Fruity Pebbles.

I wonder if you can hear me
from heaven.

Sing Jesus a song for me.
Whisper if you have to,
my prayer
to arouse our finest
psalms of freedom—
to get us over.

I'll sing for them,
blow kisses of truth,
smile a solar ballet.

I'll sing for you, angel—
God's chosen.

I'll make it,
one day like you.

The Last Song:
A Whitney Houston Original

Sing your final song.
Song of strength,
courage.
Fight to overcome
to over-make-it.

A rainbow appeared in you—
the rain did not fall anymore,
you sang the last song.

The people spoke of
a fiery voice and
troubled heart,
you blazed that trail
led right up to the gates.

I am, mostly because
you were—
that's the truth,
your spirit deep in my soul
growing up into the clouds.

JAMES B. GOLDEN

I played notes so sweet
for you to sing
open chords and
treble clefts line the
walls of your soul.

A life not wasted,
legacy unbreakable
top-heavy rhymes and
distant times
to share the gift
God gave the lady,
the last song.

No, not maybe
my heart will never
be the same—
a sun appeared in you
the light shone so bright,
it took out my eyesight.

Be with me always,
I know that you will.

I miss you already,
and much more still.

Close casket
open throne
rid the wrong—

I can't believe you're gone.

You sang the last song.

Why Are You Forcing Me To Eat Vegetables?

Getting Old Isn't For Sissies

I don't have gray hair yet
but my hairline continues to recede.
I've begun to bald,
getting old isn't for sissies.

Alzheimer's hasn't onset yet
but I always lose my keys
and what I ate last night
generally escapes me.

My excessive regimen often hibernates
and push-ups go on hiatus.
I have huge corns on the sides of my feet,
getting old isn't for sissies.

My tolerance for bullshit has decreased,
this convenience store checker is taking much
too long to bag these groceries.

I prefer smooth jazz to rough beats,
Boney James, India.Arie
no more beer pong for me.

I don't eat Top Ramen noodles and
I fall asleep watching TV,
I don't care anymore,
getting old isn't for sissies.

Sun All Over Me

I woke to the
sun all over me
gently warming my toes
filling my skin with
solar goodness.

It was the most
halcyon morning
my dishwasher rushing
roaring rapids
jet cleaning those dishes.

I'm hungry
but the pots are all dirty.

Such is the life of an
early-morning riser.

On The Occasion Of
Frank Ocean Coming Out

Hip Hop grew up today.

You came out,
clouds went away.

Lovelessness runs rampant
through artist closets.

Packed to the brim
clothes overflowing
afraid to speak
their sexual reality—
display their
God-given
identity.

Right on,
Frank Ocean.

Make Hip Hop
spin on its
spindle.

Scratch like an
80s DJ,
wear that stylus
out!

Why Are You Forcing Me To Eat Vegetables?

Mommy, please!

Don't do this to me.

No tiny bit of
me can stand to eat
another bite of veggies.

I don't care if
broccoli, cauliflower, spinach
is good for me.

I want nothing to do
with 'em.

Salad sucks!

I can't breathe when I chew
those pasty green leaves.

Attention Vegetables:
get your slimy paws
the hell away
from this mouth,
fortress of teeth.

JAMES B. GOLDEN

My taste buds absolutely
refuse to comprehend
the essential need
you have in me.

Give me noodles
or give me death.
Spaghetti, fettuchini
macaroni and cheese
not carrots or kale
and absolutely no peas.

Mommy, I swear
I'll hold my breath
until I pass all the way out
if you do this to me.

Stinky Fart

Sitting attentive in class
hoping my glasses
make me look smart,
then it starts
the guts growl to the end
and restart.

Heart begins to pound
sweat bops around
my forehead like 200 little
beads dropping on the floor
simultaneously.

The teacher was just
getting to the good part
about Picasso and
post-modern art.

I cannot
will not
let this thing take control
of me.
I have the power

the function belongs to me.
Still it seeps out like
an ever-growing tree,
blowing my belly up
like the minute-hand
at high-noon tea.

Ducking and dodging
I'm out of my seat,
stepping over comrades
trying to be discreet.
Guess I shouldn't have over-
indulged the culinary cart
bean burritos
outside the Main St. K-Mart.
Jet down the hallway
almost tripped over the
laundry cart.

Lord, please let me get there
after everyone departs.
Run into the bathroom
spread those cheeks apart
push ever so gracefully
to escape that stinky fart.

Clutter

Beguiled by
amazing new-found obscurities
flustered in an endless pile of
old newspapers
unopened telephone bills
greeting cards my nieces made
two Christmases ago.

Disoriented and confused
a little perturbed and
authentically puzzled,
ashamed this clutter
has grown to take over
my abode
my desk
my nose
smelling like old library books
and stale cheese shreds
totally complicated and
wildly mine.

Pesto Sauce

Told you I hated the
smell of it—
you spread it on
everything:
toast, tacos, jerky, salami
eggs in the morning
used on chili as frosting.

The nastiest, ghastliest,
most repudiating
sewer green pasta dressing
these eyes have ever seen.

Take your conductive hearing loss
that pesto sauce
and hang-glide off a cliff
deep into the sea.

Smell You Coming

Good perfume is like
good wine—
sweet and long lasting,
but you don't seem to
understand that much.

I close multiple doors
before you enter,
that bargain-store scent
smells up the furniture.

Oh, what alchemy has
caused your skin to
smell like this?
Seagull droppings on potpourri
and shitty daisies.

God, I must be crazy.

I should smell you coming,
not going,
but going is the only thing
I'd rather you do.

Live Supernaturally

Be unique
at all costs
fall a thousand times.

Be face-down
with ants strewn
along the carpet.

Cry
it helps.

Get up
stare obstacles down
beat it until the
white meat shows,
Baby!

Live supernaturally.

Heal sickness
with words and
spiritual medicament.

Remove doubt
there's nothing
impossible
not even walking
on water.

Marry Faith
in a dove-filled
ceremony.

Be King.

Be uniquely His
a vessel of God
with purpose and
fulfillment.

Be His,
live supernaturally.

JAMES B. GOLDEN

Groomzilla

Charles is a Groomzilla,
and he shouldn't be.

Men don't plan weddings
they show up unaffectedly.

Brides have the right to be
nervous about complimentary colors
cake and brie.

Still he roars on
beats his chest
shows his teeth.

What To Do With Cows

Squeeze tittie
jerk down
around
repeat

drain that milk
plant those feet

cows don't care for
cold-handed
massages.

Warm it up
before prodding

this has been your
cow-milking
lesson

for the inexperienced
farmer.

Play with her nipples
before the
slaughter.

Appendix

My appendix ran
away from me.

That little broken bastard
decided to break down
like a faulty engine
now my insides are
empty.

Knots all over my abdomen
like 20 pounding monkeys
bruising my core.

100,000-situps-worth sore.

A forklift running into my guts
once more.

How A Victim Convinces Himself The World Did Him Wrong At An NA Meeting

Hello, I'm Victim . . .
and I'm an addict.

      Hi Victim!

I was once one of those bubbly
ebullient-type people,
but circumstance
circumcised me.

Infidelity stole my victory
my girlfriend wore me as an accessory
Daddy never gave me the backstory
Jack Daniel's alone was too boring
Mrs. Shitzandgiggles wasn't trustworthy
she told Mom about my corduroys soaked in pee
I missed my baptism in the Red Sea
"Marsha Marsha Marsha", I'm Jan Brady
look at me I'm a victim of the school bully
I would've been loved more as a worker bee

the queen and hive would've called me Captain T
shouldn't have let you pick from my apple tree
too many missed opportunities
I have a comb-over that deserves a master's degree
the hairstylist used too much lye
I cannot see
so I don't do much work
my boss simply hates me.

I'm in 12-step recovery
trying to get back to loving me
hating everyone who did me wrong.

I'll take them on
after one more hit
of this glass-pipe
bong.

The Boy Who Lost His Grandma

Mrs. Kelley told me a scary story
about a boy and his grandma.

Crocodile tears plopping
down his cheek bones.
Mouth opened wider than
watermelons at summertime
passing air in and out
like hospital pumps
sounding sleep
snoring awake,
the boy who lost his
grandma at the fair.

Shaking, shaking violently
"someone please help me!"
Alone in a crowd of
250,000 attendees
straw hats and
frozen lemonades.

Where, my God,
where can she be?
Grandma has finally
lost me.

She did it on purpose,
I swear.

Shouldn't have made
rags of her unused weave hair,
now I'm the boy who lost his
grandma at the fair.

What I Do About Bill Collectors

Bill collectors tried
to run my life last night.
They must've called at least
two thousand times
filming messages like movie scenes,
wouldn't give them a damn thing.

There I was
on the living room patio
high-steppin'
stompin'
dancing around in the
moonlight.

Earth wouldn't shatter
for me.

I danced my collections
all away.

They faded one by one
like credits.

The popcorn was out—
end scene.

The Inside Of An Orange

Pieces

Pieces of me have
spread all along the floor.
I'm in every space and nook
searching for my
place.

I shattered 12 years ago
and stand here,
in line at Michael's
to buy my very first
glue gun.

I Need A Poem

I don't miss any of my yesterdays
hope all the yesterday's pass away.

A newness—
fresh creation.

In touch with real words
true hearts.

I need a poem to come
from my loins and
save the people from
disastrous plots.

I cannot be this emotional and
keep it locked inside
a thought box.

This insomnia is going to
leave or
it will
rot.

The Problem With Perfectionism

It's so hard to look at my fingernails
without perfecting the cuticles
or rubbing away stretch marks
with Palmers Coco Butter.
Things around the house
can never smell fusty,
that's the problem with
perfectionism.

I cannot drive a filthy car
and would surely die if ashes were left
to stain
the little compartment beneath
the stereo.

I only drink expensive wine,
my sock drawer looks like
a city map
houses neatly lined in rows like
strawberry field trenches,
I always find a disaster
in the mirror,
that's the problem with
perfectionism.

I cut my eyes at improper grammar
edit my supervisor's memos
anonymously place them back in his box
and continue on to a pricy restaurant for lunch.
I scrub floors until the color changes
then I have to retile,
that's the problem with
perfectionism.

The song is never completely written
nor the poem properly worded
sheets are still wrinkled
wine glasses aren't nearly
clear enough to sit on a shelf.
Prayer time isn't as effective anymore
apples are always eaten to the core,
love is never enough but
endless conversation can cure
the days of doing too much
planning and overextending multitasking.

Gift bags aren't appropriate wrappings
I hate napping
too much time wasted
not enough color in this prism,
that's the problem with perfectionism.

Son Of The Night

I'm a son of the night,
my skin is golden

I look just like the
inside of an orange

fruit plopping from branches
to coal-black soil
composting with time

planting my seed in the moon.

The Pen Sits Still

Quiet,
so quiet.
The pen sits still and
stares me in the face.

Can't get these still images
out of my face!

Sunlight makes streaks on my
dirty carpet floor,
accentuating the dust spots,
old black mold.

Air madly rushes through the
cracked patio wall,
slipping through my housecoat,
my drawers.

Spider journeys eventually from
upper east corner to an empty
light socket,
tip toeing around
not mumbling a sound.

If spiders could talk,
they'd have quirky stories to
tell of strange happenings
and near fatal spells.

I spun my web from the
door to the porch
and lay softly in it,
my quiet right with it.

Granny's Sick

Granny's sick
and the baby's bathwater
is cold.

Took her mind down to the
watering hole,
fished with its strings,
baited with aged
memory glands
disrobed.

Granny's sick
and the tides have turned,
planted her deep in the
earth's below
to teach a thing or two
to unloving souls,
a minute closer to
heavenly adventures
evermore.

Granny's sick
and the baby's bathwater
is cold.

Give me back my mind
give me back my soul.

I'll Wash Dishes

you do, you do,
buckle my little black shoe
eat from a tiny little saucer
sit at a little pink plastic table
in your disheveled
little room.

toys toys toys
lined all around
up and down the walls
and floors
and cabinetry.

always knew your
imaginary food would taste
best served
so sweetly on toast.

I'll wash dishes,
you will too
but I'll take the suds side
you'll dry em cool.

did not know,
did not know
he would touch your
virginity so.

took away those scrumptious
invisible meals too,
turned your lights off
little girl blue.

Clarity

I'm okay
not knowing.
Being alone in the dark
doesn't scare me.
Most things I care not to know,
the origins centers
that from whence they grow.
As I give this
it's said with all sincerity

Clarity
Oh Clarity,
don't waste your time
on me.

Spend time with the skeptics,
those who seek concept familiarity.
Walk around nose in book
deciphering theory irregularities.
Stick close to those with
limb dexterity,
I'll always walk with a
certain peculiarity.

Clarity
Oh Clarity,
don't waste your time
on me.

Build fences around men
with grand-enough austerity,
he who seeks deliverance
from ample modernity.
I'll sip slowly and absorb
my easy regularity

Clarity
Oh Clarity,
I'll shoot if you
come any closer.

Bang ! Bang!

Rest in peace.

James B. Golden

My Mommy Taught Me

Every Friday night we waltzed
freeways to street lanes
in search of the hardwood
oval shape where
my mommy taught me
to skate.

Sam and I followed her
wheel tracks
dusted and deserted
spinning around the rink
in ovals
trying hard not to
spill down to the ground
embarrassing myself
in front of the
pretty girls.

My mommy taught me
to skate upright
into deserted territory
outside of apathy.

When A Granddaughter Loves Her Poppy

Grandpa was too boring
and Granddaddy too much to spell
Grampy wasn't good enough
and Papa not so swell

I preferred Poppy
and always loved him so,
even the moons and winds
had to sit below.

I went to you—
then you were gone
train smoke billowing away
in the distance.

Poppy sprung up to
ancestral waters,
arisen like yeast in mama's
Sunday morning biscuits
and southern caramel cake.

Wish I could bake you again
or once more taste.

There's nothing sweeter
than when a granddaughter
loves her Poppy.

Just A Lamp

Someone once told me
an unrecognized lamp in a room
is just a lamp.

Well,
my father isn't a lamp.
He don't flicker off and on like
a nightlight.

Jared

You've dawdled around my mind
and up many stairs ran
I've loved you more than
I can stand.

Cruelties children shouldn't have
the capacity to face,
toddler abandonment
parental shame—
drugs around the house,
sex and violent
happenstances.

You've been a prince
and mine so grand,
I've loved you more than
I can stand.

Brilliant beyond words
a true musician's delivery
Black baby boy with a
teddy bear heart,
you've assumed many roles
like a name brand,
I've love you more than
I can stand.

The day we met
promised myself I'd be the
appropriate father for you
show you how to stand
on giant shoulders so grand
a perfectly beautiful
God-blessed young man.

You've been my heart
and I've always been yours
a connection deeper than oceans
refined-pearl pure,
beyond utterances.

You'll always be my little man
I've loved you fiercely, purposefully
more than life allows a man,
I've loved you more than
I can stand.

The Love Suite:
Make You Fall In Love

I'm gonna make you fall in love
with me.

These words will get in your guts
eventually.

Swim all around up in there like
piranhas chomping you to bits.

When I speak,
my tongue is a beast
ready to tear up your face
to a stripped down pulp.

I'm gonna make you fall in love
with my lyric.

Sweeter than dried honeycomb—
Splenda sweet.

Love,
please fall in love
with me.

Sex, Growing Inside Of Me

I burn down every night
awaiting the release,
get this stuff out,
please.

Sex, growing inside of me
tickling loins
igniting my bloodstream

protruding lips kiss my
shoulder softly
head on pillow
watching the double coat
dry on the wall.

Raw

It smelled like sewer
in there
and your sheets
were dirty,
that first night
with you
was unearthing.

The air was raw and
must bred itself
over and over
on our skins.

We were one at times
and none most times
legs entwined
at once you made me
cum twice.

I climbed the bedposts
for you
made the sun and moon
confused.
Lord have mercy,
that first night
with you
was unearthing.

You were mine
that night
and I was yours
alike
we did not fight
we did not lie.

Poison

My adult-life through
I've been snake bitten by you.
Tossed my availability around
with olive oil
and fried it to a
golden crisp.

I crusted over for you.

Bud ashes and beer residue
build up in your
little wooden box.

You carry it like a
good luck charm
sparking it whenever lost.

Over me.
Over me?

You'd choose poison
over me.

I gave you my sophoric sex
and rose dozens
even when money dried up.
Flew you high in a balloon,
tied up and parasailed for you.

I'll finally let go
your behavior will get old
and rot away at the legs
it'll be all pain
until you learn to stop playing
video games
drinking your life away.

Poison
Poison
Over me.
Out of me.

Puke On My Love

Another person
had to tell me you were
messin' around.

After I'd given you
all my secrets
revealed my insecurities
truthed my biggest lies.

And what did you do?
but puke on my love.

You left me out to thaw like
frozen meat before work,
and I'll burn
when they put me on
those coals.

Heartbeat

I thought I already loved you most,
then I saw you dancing
in your underwear
to "How Will I Know".

Fell deeper in love with you.

I saw tribes dancing,
stamping up dust and
waving arms around fluidly
like the skies were close enough
to touch.

Your smile was from outer-space,
bringing me to my knees with giggles.

I loved you most that day,
you danced my boogie
away.

What Am I Supposed To Do Without You?

It's been three days and the sun hasn't emerged yet
night's inside me, no sight of the blue.

What am I supposed to do without you?

Watch characters fall in love all day?

Live like I'll stay forever
or die every night
on my own?

Send me to Disneyland.

James B. Golden

I Am King

It's 3 AM again
and I've convinced myself
that I am king.
Cerebral enough to
choose my destiny.

Walking on clouds up high
away from the insignificance
of modernity.

I filled a glass with
lovely tears,
my cup runneth over.

Opened my chest up
to the winds
and carried away
ancient sorrows.

No longer worried
about tomorrow.

God gave me the life and will
to breathe.

I've made it through the broken
fragmented glass,
risen up from the ash.

I am the very best me.
I am king.

What's Next

Sacred tomorrows
grown-up trees
beach sand erosion
handsome seashells
long aimless walks
fluid mentality
wild open midnights
decreased skin elasticity
salt 'n pepper hair
nameless adventures
God-children galore
endless presents
camping with smores
acid reflux and abysmal indigestion
sleepless nights
protruding midsection
floundering sonnets
purposeful blessings
redolent smells
millions in sales
happiest mind
thrift store finds
wisdom to last
beyond the times.

Can't Take That Away

The parents gave me
confidence—
I know I can
do anything

The great experimenter of life
ready to duel it out
prepared to fight
to make the best of my days
and live wildly without chains.

I'm alive today
and you can't
take that away.

What I Know For Sure

There is a God
somewhere near the rainbow top.

He frolics with the weather
potting sunshine in darkness.

Only one life is
given us.
It will either
sink or float.
Life is a
row boat.

There are no emergency
exits on earth.
We will all die
in an emergency,
peaceful or not.

Heaven definitely exists
especially when people
use love for
oars.

Regardless,
Black kids
row through more
obstacles than others.
Their boats are likely
hazardous,
needing repair.

The inside of an orange
is sweeter than anything known.
Textured little juice
pockets squeeze sunshine
from God to our taste buds.

The sun will set
even on mighty, mighty
Los Angeles September days.
The coolness
a kiss
softer than pink
cotton candy,

but what I know for sure
is
we have meaning,
our lives are purposed.

No mistakes here.

There is a God.

The Artist Poem

I am Artist.

I dance around
an elephant stamping the Cupid Shuffle
down the Sahara
embellishing the sun's arrival with a foot praisin'
South African step routine.

I dance rhythmically like a
Nicholas Brother
hot pants James and
Michael's Smooth Criminal
all at once.

I am Artist.

The records spin in the forayer
Stevie's Innervisions exposed and coupled
with a Mary J. Blige tape in springtime.

I drown in Rihanna, fist-pumping
"we found love in a hopeless place",
a yellow diamond in the light
rain falling over my umbrella ella ella eh eh eh
Aretha's Bridge Over Troubled Water.

I am Artist.

I meld melodies somewhat Rachelle Farrell and Lalah Hathaway
Jody Watley posters taped to a sophomore
Black boy's bedroom ceiling.

I run faders up for Nas' Illmatic
automatically the most recognizable portrait we have
to offer for auction.

Watch me sample Brooklyn with Puff Daddy
push play for Macy Gray
make love to organ pipes
giving a Ray Charles head-throw.

Dubbing a Prince Darling Nikki
strumming up symphonious selective delicacies
chocolate to the ear.

I am Artist.

I've written 42 complicated Saturday nights
dialogued 27 Jesse B. Simple conversations with my eyes closed
words brought to life and tapping to "Jesus Is On The Main Line, Tell
Him What You Want"
Sunday morning souls slain in the spirit.

Langston laid hands and
sent me on down south to sip wine in Zora's backyard
where God's eyes watched patiently.

Nikki and Sonia sketched passion for me
I traced them on cardstock,
slept with their whiskey-stained lyrics rising up-down
atop the back of a drunken passer-out.

I am Artist,
speaker of truth
philosopher to the skies
conducting star alignment.

Nina Simone and Bruce Nugent
Jayne Cortez's celebration of the dead rapist punk
Lorraine Hansberry's A Raisin In The Sun
a dream materializing
giant canvas where paint runs.

I am Dizzy Gilespie, Count Basie, John Legend, Kanye West.
I am Melvin Tolson, June Jordan, Toni Morrison, Amiri Baracka.

I am this poem.

Anita Baker, a bit Mariah Carey, Billie's "Don't Explain"
Tina's "Private Dancer".

I'm a dancer for this generation.
A Fatimah Robinson, Aaliyah Haughton, Judith Jamison, an Alvin Ailey.

I dream wildly Cee-Lo, sound somewhat Whitney Houstonian
lonely violin in the Philharmonic, woodwind surfing a Santa Cruz
blow.
I am Spike Lee in the B.K.
Julie Dash, Tyler Perry, a November chill's August Wilson
David E. Talbert—staged symphony.

I am Ben Harper, Lenny Kravitz, Lauryn Hill, Corrine Bailey Rae
supremely John Coltrane
singing the sax
painting without numbers
telling stories of revolutions passed
trilogies of Blackness rooted deeper than a Live Oak tree
hard as day-old biscuits
soft as Granny's pancake batter and rose-scented oil.

I am Artist.
Sacrificed lamb of the streets.
Philosophized, scrutinized
at times empty
in others
a pot of gumbo's full.

Human
Being

I am Artist.
I am Me.

JAMES B. GOLDEN

Notes

Page 3: "Son Of Obama" contains a portion of Psalms 23:5, one of the most emotive Bible verses.

Page 7: "An Erykah Badu Poem" entwines multiple songs from Badu's catalogue including "Orange Moon", "A.D. 2000", "On & On", "Honey", and "Back In The Day".

Page 15: "They Don't Have To" was written after a conversation about race and gas stations with Sydnie.

Page 16: "Freedom's Gate" was written for NAACP, SNCC, SCLC, The Black Panther Party For Self Defense, and all other coalitions for equality.

Page 21: "A Fine Composition" is dedicated to the memory of our dearest brother, Nick Ashford. The poem incorporates "Remember Me", written by Nick for Diana Ross.

Page 24: "Rahsaan's Blues" is written for amazing Soul vocalist Rahsaan Patterson.

Page 43: "Pesto Sauce". You know who you are. *I bet you think this song is about you.*

Page 45: "Live Supernaturally" was inspired by P.T. and Matthew 10:6-9.

Page 49: "Appendix" was written for Willie.

Page 64: "Granny's Sick" is dedicated to my grandmothers Hazel and Henrietta, who are battling the horrors of Alzheimer's disease.

Page 65: The opening lines of "I'll Wash Dishes" references "Daddy" by Sylvia Plath.

Page 69: "My Mommy Taught Me" was written for my mother. We used to take trips to Monterey's Del Monte Skating Rink every Friday.

Page 70: "When A Granddaughter Loves Her Poppy" is dedicated to my dear friend Tiffany.

Page 72: "Jared" is a note to one of the most amazing young men I've ever had the pleasure of knowing.

Page 81: "Heartbeat" references "How Will I Know" (1985), a song recorded by Whitney Houston.

Page 83: "I Am King" references Psalms 23:5.

Acknowledgements

"For free is not merely to cast off one's chains,
but to live in a way that respects and enhances the
freedom of others."
—Nelson Mandela

Thank you to the most-high God for these gifts of the dust.

The author wishes to thank everyone who workshopped *The Inside Of An Orange*. Thanks to Carroll J. Brown for the amazing art work on the cover.

Thank you to James and Valerie Golden, family, mentors, muses, and friends. A humongous thanks to Carrington Baber, the author's research and personal assistant.

A special thanks goes out to the entire **I Read Poetry** campaign. It's time to start reading again, promoting love and understanding to this world.

Dedication

This book is offered in memory of the greatest artist I've ever known, the dynamic *Whitney Houston*. You've been a central part of my life since I was 5 years old.

Your gift of artistic perfection will inspire us for centuries. Your love for fellow artists has been a godsend to us all. Getting the opportunity to stand before you as you sang your final song at Kelly Price's Grammy party the day before you passed was one of the defining moments of my life. *"Yes, Jesus Loves Me"* never sounded more handsome.

It is not conjecture—you are simply the best . . .and no one has ever done it better. Lady, your spirit lives on in me.

I believe that our spirits are connected eternally, and that you've implanted wisdom in me from the greatest love of all.

Whitney, you declared "I was not meant to break", and you didn't. You stood tall and remained resilient throughout the most painful times—a true victor.

Your voice was silk. It was water—fluid, everlasting, nourishing. You fed us the soul and spirit we longed to know for our entire lives. I only hope to inspire people they way you did.

Thank you for the music.
Thank you, God . . . for the life.

> *"If I should die this very day . . . don't cry, 'cause on earth we wasn't meant to stay. No matter what people say . . . I'll be waiting for you after the judgment day."*
> **—"My Love Is Your Love", 1998**

God bless you dear angel.

Love,

James

About The Author

James B. Golden was born and raised in Salinas, California, and received his M.P.A. and B.A. in English and Pan-African Studies Arts & Literature from California State University, Northridge. He has edited Kapu-Sens Literary Journal and the Hip Hop Think Tank Journal. He is the author of the 2012 NAACP Image Award winning book *Afro Clouds & Nappy Rain,* and the Langston Hughes Award winning book *Sweet Potato Pie Underneath The Sun's Broiler.*

Golden lectures around the country on topics including: creative writing, Hip Hop, Black-male feminism, and pop culture. He currently lives in Los Angeles, where he is a music and pop-culture journalist. His articles have appeared in such periodicals as VIBE, Clutch Magazine, Jazz Times, and Our Weekly.

Golden has appeared on several radio and television shows, including The Young Turks.

For more information:
www.JamesBGolden.com
Follow James: @jamesbgolden